THE DIARY OF A
YOUNG GIRL

Anne Frank

Spark Publishing
A Division of Barnes & Noble
120 Fifth Avenue
New York, NY 10011
www.sparknotes.com

ISBN-13: 978-1-5866-3457-5
ISBN-10: 1-5866-3457-7

Please submit changes or report errors to www.sparknotes.com/errors.

Printed and bound in The United States.

7 9 10 8 6

Introduction: Stopping to Buy Sparknotes on a Snowy Evening

Whose words these are you *think* you know.
Your paper's due tomorrow, though;
We're glad to see you stopping here
To get some help before you go.

Lost your course? You'll find it here.
Face tests and essays without fear.
Between the words, good grades at stake:
Get great results throughout the year.

Once school bells caused your heart to quake
As teachers circled each mistake.
Use SparkNotes and no longer weep,
Ace every single test you take.

Yes, books are lovely, dark, and deep,
But only what you grasp you keep,
With hours to go before you sleep,
With hours to go before you sleep.

Contents

NOTE: This SparkNote refers to *The Diary of a Young Girl: Anne Frank*, The Definitive Edition, published by Bantam Books in 1997. This edition of the work includes the most up-to-date version of the diary; any editions published before 1991 do not include the diary selections that were originally removed by Otto Frank.

CONTEXT

Perhaps the most famous personal account of the Holocaust, *The Diary of Anne Frank* was written in Amsterdam, the Netherlands, between 1942 and 1944. The Franks were a Jewish family originally from Germany, where Anne was born in 1929. Anne's father, Otto, had come from a wealthy background, but his family's fortune was lost after World War I.

In 1933 the Franks moved to the Netherlands to escape Nazi persecution. The family lived in relative peace until 1940, when Germany occupied the Netherlands and imposed stringent anti-Semitic laws. These new measures prohibited Jews from riding streetcars, forced Jews to attend separate schools, imposed boycotts of Jewish-owned businesses, and required Jews to wear yellow stars to identify themselves as Jewish. The quality of life of even highly assimilated Jews, like the Franks, became precarious. Within two years after these anti-Semitic laws were imposed, many Jews in the Netherlands were harassed, arrested, and sent to concentration camps where they were herded together and killed. The Franks and other well-connected families were able to heed warning signs in time to make arrangements to go into hiding. This decision put their own lives and the lives of those who cared for them at great risk.

Anne was thrilled to receive a diary on her thirteenth birthday and expressed hope that it would become her one trusted confidant. She immediately began filling her diary with details of her life, including descriptions of her friends, boys she liked, and events at school. Less than one month after she began documenting her relatively carefree childhood, Anne and her family were suddenly forced into hiding.

Margot, Anne's sixteen-year-old sister, had been "called up" by the Gestapo, Germany's brutal secret-police force. It was common knowledge among Jews that being called up meant eventually being sent to one of the notorious concentration camps. The Franks were relatively prepared, since they had been sending furniture and provisions to a secret annex in Otto's office building in anticipation of the Gestapo. The Franks and another family, the van Daans, had arranged to share the annex while some of Otto's non-Jewish colleagues agreed to look after the families. The Franks later invited one more person, Mr. Dussel, to share their annex.

While they were in hiding, the Franks used a radio to keep up with news from the war, and Anne frequently wrote in her diary about events that caught her attention. These bits—speeches by Winston Churchill; the advances by the British—provide a vivid historical context for Anne's personal thoughts and feelings.

The Gestapo finally arrested Anne and her family on August 4, 1944. Two secretaries who worked in the building found the books containing Anne's diary entries strewed over the floor of the annex. The secretaries handed over the diaries to Miep Gies, an assistant in Otto's office. Miep held the diary, unread, in a desk drawer. When the war ended in 1945, Miep delivered the diary to Otto Frank, who had survived the horrors of the Auschwitz concentration camp. Anne and Margot died of typhus at the Bergen-Belsen concentration camp in February or March of 1945. Their mother died of hunger and exhaustion in Auschwitz in January 1945. The van Daans and Mr. Dussel also perished in the camps.

Otto Frank knew of his daughter's wish to become a published writer. Anne originally kept the diary only as a private memoir, but in 1944 she changed her mind after hearing a broadcast by Gerrit Boklestein, a member of the Dutch government in exile. Boklestein declared his hope to publish Dutch people's accounts of the war, which inspired Anne to think about the possibility of writing for posterity. In addition to her diary, Anne wrote several fables and short stories with an eye toward publishing them someday. She also had thoughts of becoming a journalist.

Mr. Frank reviewed the diary and selected passages, keeping in mind constraints on length and appropriateness for a young-adult audience. He also left out certain passages that he considered unflattering to his late wife and the other residents of the annex. When Mr. Frank died in 1980, the Anne Frank Foundation in Basel, Switzerland, inherited the copyright to the diary. A new, complete edition, which restored the passages Mr. Frank left out of the original edition, was published in 1991.

Plot Overview

NNE'S DIARY BEGINS on her thirteenth birthday, June 12, 1942, and ends shortly after her fifteenth. At the start of her diary, Anne describes fairly typical girlhood experiences, writing about her friendships with other girls, her crushes on boys, and her academic performance at school. Because anti-Semitic laws forced Jews into separate schools, Anne and her older sister, Margot, attended the Jewish Lyceum in Amsterdam.

The Franks had moved to the Netherlands in the years leading up to World War II to escape persecution in Germany. After the Germans invaded the Netherlands in 1940, the Franks were forced into hiding. With another family, the van Daans, and an acquaintance, Mr. Dussel, they moved into a small secret annex above Otto Frank's office where they had stockpiled food and supplies. The employees from Otto's firm helped hide the Franks and kept them supplied with food, medicine, and information about the outside world.

The residents of the annex pay close attention to every development of the war by listening to the radio. Some bits of news catch Anne's attention and make their way into her diary, providing a vivid historical context for her personal thoughts. The adults make optimistic bets about when the war will end, and their mood is severely affected by Allied setbacks or German advances. Amsterdam is devastated by the war during the two years the Franks are in hiding. All of the city's residents suffer, since food becomes scarce and robberies more frequent.

Anne often writes about her feelings of isolation and loneliness. She has a tumultuous relationship with the adults in the annex, particularly her mother, whom she considers lacking in love and affection. She adores her father, but she is frequently scolded and criticized by Mr. and Mrs. van Daan and Mr. Dussel. Anne thinks that her sister, Margot, is smart, pretty, and agreeable, but she does not feel close to her and does not write much about her. Anne eventually develops a close friendship with Peter van Daan, the teenage boy in the annex. Mr. Frank does not approve, however, and the intensity of Anne's infatuation begins to lessen.

Anne matures considerably throughout the course of her diary entries, moving from detailed accounts of basic activities to deeper, more profound thoughts about humanity and her own personal nature. She finds it difficult to understand why the Jews are being singled out and persecuted. Anne also confronts her own identity. Though she considers herself to be German, her German citizenship has been revoked, and though she calls Holland her home, many of the Dutch have turned against the Jews. Anne feels a tremendous solidarity with her aggrieved people, and yet at the same time she wants to be seen as an individual rather than a member of a persecuted group.

During the two years recorded in her diary, Anne deals with confinement and deprivation, as well as the complicated and difficult issues of growing up in the brutal circumstances of the Holocaust. Her diary describes a struggle to define herself within this climate of oppression. Anne's diary ends without comment on August 1, 1944, the end of a seemingly normal day that leaves us with the expectation of seeing another entry on the next page. However, the Frank family is betrayed to the Nazis and arrested on August 4, 1944. Anne's diary, the observations of an imaginative, friendly, sometimes petty, and rather normal teenage girl, comes to an abrupt and silent end.

Otto Frank is the family's sole survivor, and he recovers Anne's diary from Miep. He decides to fulfill Anne's wishes by publishing the diary. Anne's diary becomes a condemnation of the unimaginable horror of the Holocaust, and one of the few accounts that describe it from a young person's perspective.

Since Anne's diary is a true personal account of a life in hiding, it is inappropriate to analyze it as a novel or other work of fiction. Parts of the diary were intended for public view, but others clearly were not. To appreciate and interpret the diary, it is necessary to consider its horrible context, World War II and the Holocaust, before any discussion of plot development or thematic content.

CHARACTER LIST

Anne Frank The author of the diary. Anne was born on June 12, 1929, in Frankfurt, Germany, and was four years old when her father moved to Holland to find a better place for the family to live. She is very intelligent and perceptive, and she wants to become a writer. Anne grows from an innocent, tempestuous, precocious, and somewhat petty teenage girl to an empathetic and sensitive thinker at age fifteen. Anne dies of typhus in the concentration camp at Bergen-Belsen in late February or early March of 1945.

Margot Frank Anne's older sister. Margot was born in Frankfurt in 1926. She receives little attention in Anne's diary, and Anne does not provide a real sense of Margot's character. Anne thinks that Margot is pretty, smart, emotional, and everyone's favorite. However, Anne and Margot do not form a close bond, and Margot mainly appears in the diary when she is the cause of jealousy or anger. She dies of typhus in the concentration camp a few days before Anne does.

Otto Frank Anne's father. Otto is practical and kind, and Anne feels a particular kinship to him. He was born on May 12, 1889, into a wealthy Frankfurt family, but the family's international-banking business collapsed during the German economic depression that followed World War I. After the Nazis came to power in Germany, Otto moved to Amsterdam in 1933 to protect his family from persecution. There he made a living selling chemical products and provisions until the family was forced into hiding in 1942. Otto is the only member of the family to survive the war, and he lives until 1980.

Edith Frank Anne's mother. Edith Hollander was originally from Aachen, Germany, and she married Otto in 1925. Anne feels little closeness or sympathy with her mother, and the two have a very tumultuous relationship. Anne thinks her mother is too sentimental and critical. Edith dies of hunger and exhaustion in the concentration camp at Auschwitz in January 1945.

Mr. van Daan The father of the family that hides in the annex along with the Franks and who had worked with Otto Frank as an herbal specialist in Amsterdam. Mr. van Daan's actual name is Hermann van Pels, but Anne calls him Mr. van Daan in the diary. According to Anne, he is intelligent, opinionated, pragmatic, and somewhat egotistical. Mr. van Daan is temperamental, speaks his mind openly, and is not afraid to cause friction, especially with his wife, with whom he fights frequently and openly. He dies in the gas chambers at Auschwitz in October or November of 1944.

Mrs. van Daan Mr. van Daan's wife. Her actual name is Auguste van Pels, but Anne calls her Petronella van Daan in her diary. Anne initially describes Mrs. van Daan as a friendly, teasing woman, but later calls her an instigator. She is a fatalist and can be petty, egotistical, flirtatious, stingy, and disagreeable. Mrs. van Daan frequently complains about the family's situation— criticism that Anne does not admire or respect. Mrs. van Daan does not survive the war, but the exact date of her death is unknown.

Peter van Daan The teenage son of the van Daans, whose real name is Peter van Pels. Anne first sees Peter as obnoxious, lazy, and hypersensitive, but later they become close friends. Peter is quiet, timid, honest, and sweet to Anne, but he does not share her strong convictions. During their time in the annex, Anne and Peter develop a romantic attraction, which Mr. Frank discourages. Peter is Anne's first kiss, and he is her one confidant and source of affection and attention in the annex. Peter dies on May 5, 1945, at the concentration camp at Mauthausen, only three days before the camp was liberated.

Albert Dussel A dentist and an acquaintance of the Franks who hides with them in the annex. His real name is Fritz Pfeffer, but Anne calls him Mr. Dussel in the diary. Anne finds Mr. Dussel particularly difficult to deal with because he shares a room with her, and she suffers the brunt of his odd personal hygiene habits, pedantic lectures, and controlling tendencies. Mr. Dussel's wife is a Christian, so she does not go into hiding, and he is separated from her. He dies on December 20, 1944, at the Neuengamme concentration camp.

Mr. Kugler A man who helps hide the Franks in the annex. Victor Kugler is arrested along with Kleiman in 1944 but escapes in 1945. He immigrates to Canada in 1955 and dies in Toronto in 1981. Mr. Kugler is also referred to as Mr. Kraler.

Mr. Kleiman Another man who helps the Franks hide. Johannes Kleiman is arrested in 1944 but released because of poor health. He remains in Amsterdam until his death in 1959. Mr. Kleiman is also referred to as Mr. Koophuis.

Bep Voskuijl A worker in Otto Frank's office. Elizabeth (Bep) Voskuijl helps the family by serving as a liaison to the outside world. She remains in Amsterdam until her death in 1983.

Mr. Voskuijl Bep's father.

Miep Gies A secretary at Otto's office who helps the Franks hide. After the Franks are arrested, she stows the diary away in a desk drawer and keeps it there, unread, until Otto's return in 1945. She is still living in Amsterdam.

Jan Gies   Miep's husband. He dies in 1993.

Hanneli   Anne's school friend. The Nazis arrest her early in the war.

Peter Schiff   The love of Anne's life from the sixth grade. Peter Schiff is a boy one year older than Anne. She has dreams about him while in the annex. Peter Schiff is also referred to as Peter Wessel.

Hello Silberberg   A boy with whom Anne has an innocent, though romantic relationship before she goes into hiding. Hello is also referred to as Harry Goldberg.

ANALYSIS OF MAJOR CHARACTERS

ANNE FRANK

When Anne Frank is given a diary for her thirteenth birthday, she immediately fills it with the details of her life: descriptions of her friends, boys who like her, and her classes at school. Anne finds comfort writing in her diary because she feels she has difficulty opening up to her friends and therefore has no true confidants. Anne also records her perceptions of herself. She does not think she is pretty, but she is confident that her personality and other good traits make up for it. Through her writing, Anne comes across as playful and comical but with a serious side.

Anne's diary entries show from the outset that she is content and optimistic despite the threats and danger that her family faces. The tone and substance of her writing change considerably while she is in hiding. Anne is remarkably forthright and perceptive at the beginning of the diary, but as she leaves her normal childhood behind and enters the dire and unusual circumstances of the Holocaust, she becomes more introspective and thoughtful.

During her first year in the annex, Anne struggles with the adults, who constantly criticize her behavior and consider her "exasperating." Anne feels extremely lonely and in need of kindness and affection, which she feels her mother is incapable of providing. She also wrestles with her inner self and considers what type of person she wants to become as she enters womanhood. Anne tries to understand her identity in the microcosm of the annex and attempts to understand the workings of the cruel world outside. As she matures, Anne comes to long not for female companionship, but intimacy with a male counterpart. She becomes infatuated with Peter, the van Daan's teenage son, and comes to consider him a close friend, confidant, and eventually an object of romantic desire.

In her final diary entries, Anne is particularly lucid about the changes she has undergone, her ambitions, and how her experience is changing her. She has a clear perspective of how she has matured during their time in the annex, from an insolent and obstinate girl to

9

a more emotionally independent young woman. Anne begins to think about her place in society as a woman, and her plans for overcoming the obstacles that have defeated the ambitions of women from previous generations, such as her mother. Anne continues to struggle with how she can be a good person when there are so many obstacles in her world. She writes eloquently about her confusion over her identify, raising the question of whether she will consider herself Dutch, as she hears that the Dutch have become anti-Semitic. Anne thinks philosophically about the nature of war and humanity and about her role as a young Jewish girl in a challenging world. From her diary, it is clear that she had the potential to become an engaging, challenging, and sophisticated writer.

OTTO FRANK

In Anne's eyes, Mr. Frank is one of the kindest, smartest, most gentle and thoughtful fathers imaginable. He almost always supports Anne and frequently takes her side during family arguments. He is generous, kind, and levelheaded, while the other adults in the annex can be stingy, harsh, and emotional. Unlike Mr. Dussel, for example, Mr. Frank always tries to save the best food for the children and takes the smallest portion for himself.

Anne feels a special closeness to her father, since she sees herself as more similar to him than to her mother or sister. Anne continually tries to impress her father, live up to his expectations, and obey his wishes. However, when she begins a close relationship with Peter, her father deems it inappropriate, and he asks her to stop visiting Peter in the upstairs part of the annex. Anne is very hurt that her father is so conservative, protective, and secretive about sexuality, and she is upset that he does not approve of her relationship. Out of respect for her father and in an attempt to please him, Anne begins to spend less time with Peter.

Otto was a smart, resourceful, and caring father, as well as a talented businessman. He had a strong character and was clearly the head of the Frank household. The only resident of the annex to survive the war, Otto remained in Auschwitz until it was liberated by Russian troops in 1945. He returned to Holland, where he receives Anne's diary. He remained in Holland until 1953, when he moved to Basel, Switzerland, to join his sister's family. He married another Auschwitz survivor and devoted the rest of his life to promoting Anne's diary.

EDITH FRANK

Anne has very little sympathy for her mother during their tumultuous years in the annex, and she has few kind words to say about her, particularly in the earlier entries. Anne feels that her mother is cold, critical, and uncaring, that they have very little in common, and that her mother does not know how to show love to her children. Like Margot, Mrs. Frank is mentioned almost exclusively in instances when she is the source of Anne's anger and frustration. Anne rarely comments on her mother's positive traits.

Later in her diary, however, Anne attempts to look at her mother's life as a wife and mother from a more objective viewpoint. As Anne gets older and gains a clearer perspective, she begins to regret her quick, petty judgments of her mother. Anne has more sympathetic feelings for Mrs. Frank and begins to realize how Mrs. Frank's gender and entrapment in the annex have created many obstacles for her. Despite her new perspective, Anne continues to feel estranged from her sentimental, critical mother and irrevocably deems her unfit. It seems that Mrs. Frank's inability to provide emotional support for her daughter stems in part from the stress and pain of the persecution and forced confinement. Because the diary consists of only Anne's thoughts and perspectives, we are never able to gain much insight into Mrs. Frank's own personal thoughts or feelings.

CHARACTER ANALYSIS

Themes, Motifs & Symbols

Themes

Themes are the fundamental and often universal ideas explored in a literary work.

The Loneliness of Adolescence

Anne Frank's perpetual feeling of being lonely and misunderstood provides the impetus for her dedicated diary writing and colors many of the experiences she recounts. Even in her early diary entries, in which she writes about her many friends and her lively social life, Anne expresses gratitude that the diary can act as a confidant with whom she can share her innermost thoughts. This might seem an odd sentiment from such a playful, amusing, and social young girl, but Anne explains that she is never comfortable discussing her inner emotions, even around close friends. Despite her excitement over developing into a woman, and despite the specter of war surrounding her, Anne nonetheless finds that she and her friends talk only about trivial topics.

We learn later in the diary that neither Mrs. Frank nor Margot offers much to Anne in the way of emotional support. Though Anne feels very connected to her father and derives strength and encouragement from him, he is not a fitting confidant for a thirteen-year-old girl. Near the end of her diary, Anne shares a quotation she once read with which she strongly agrees: "Deep down, the young are lonelier than the old." Because young people are less able than adults to define or express their needs clearly, they are more likely to feel lonely, isolated, and misunderstood. Living as a Jew in an increasingly anti-Jewish society, in cramped and deprived circumstances, heightens the isolation Anne feels and complicates her struggle for identity.

Anne occasionally turns to the cats that live in the annex for affection. Noticing that Peter van Daan also plays with the cats, Anne speculates that he must also suffer from a lack of affection. Anne's observation softens her view of Peter, whom she once considered obnoxious and lazy, and these thoughts cause her to think that they might have something in common. Their ensuing friendship and budding romance stave off their feelings of loneliness. Margot, who like the other members of the annex witnesses the changing nature of Anne and Peter's relationship, expresses her jealousy that Anne has found a confidant. Evidently, Anne is not the only one in the annex suffering from the deprivation of friends.

Feelings of loneliness and isolation also play out in the larger scheme of the annex. All the inhabitants feel anxious, fearful, and stressed because of their circumstances, yet no one wants to burden the others with such depressing feelings. As a result, the residents become impatient with one another over trivial matters and never address their deeper fears or worries. This constant masking and repression of serious emotions creates isolation and misunderstanding between all the residents of the annex.

THE INWARD VERSUS THE OUTWARD SELF

Anne frequently expresses her conviction that there are "two Annes": the lively, jovial, public Anne whom people find amusing or exasperating; and the sentimental, private Anne whom only she truly knows. As she comes to understand her actions and motivations better over the course of her writing, Anne continually refers to this aggravating split between her inward and outward character.

Anne is aware of this dichotomy from a young age. In her early diary entries she explains that though she has many friends and acquaintances, she feels she does not have one person to whom she can really open up. She regrets that she does not share her true self with her friends or family. Anne expresses frustration that she does not know how to share her feelings with others, and she fears that she is vulnerable to attacks on her character. When her relationship with Peter begins, Anne wonders whether he will be the first one to see through the outer, public Anne and find her true self beneath.

Anne struggles with her two selves throughout the diary, trying to be honest and genuine, while at the same time striving to fit in with the rest of the group and not create too much friction. On January 22, 1944, Anne asks a question—"Can you tell me why people go to such lengths to hide their real selves?"—that suggests she realizes she is not alone in hiding her true feelings and fears. With this realization, Anne starts to read into other people's behavior more deeply and starts to think about their true but hidden motivations.

In her final diary entry, on August 1, 1944, Anne continues to grapple with the difference between her self-perception and how she presents herself to others. She arrives at a greater resolve to be true to herself and not to fold her heart inside out so only the bad parts show.

Anne's inner struggle mirrors the larger circumstances of the war. Both the residents of the annex and the Dutch people who help them are forced to hide themselves from the public. They must take on a different identity in public to protect their livelihood because their true identities and actions would make them targets of persecution. This is yet another manifestation of the hypocrisy of identity that Anne is trying to come to terms with in her diary.

GENEROSITY AND GREED IN WARTIME

Anne's diary demonstrates that war brings out both the best and the worst traits in people. Two characteristics in particular become prominent defining poles of character in the annex—generosity and greed. The group's livelihood depends on the serious and continual risks taken by their Dutch keepers, who are generous with food, money, and any other resources they can share.

Although the annex is hardly luxurious, the Franks and van Daans feel their situation is better than that of the thousands of Jews who are in mortal danger outside. As a result, they extend Mr. Dussel an invitation to join them and to share their limited resources—an act of true generosity. The fact that Mr. Dussel accepts the others' offer but never makes any attempt to acknowledge or reciprocate their generosity might be attributed to the extreme circumstances. More likely, however, is that Mr. Dussel is the kind of person in whom hardship brings out the qualities of greed and selfishness. Indeed, the two people Anne most reviles, Mr. Dussel and Mrs. van Daan, share the tendency to look out for themselves far more than to look out for others.

Generosity and greed also come to bear on Anne's feelings of guilt about being in hiding. Although by the end of their time in the annex the residents have practically run out of food, Anne feels lucky to have escaped the fate of her friends who were sent to concentration camps. She struggles with the idea that perhaps she and her family could have been more generous and could have shared their resources with more people. While Mr. Dussel and Mrs. van Daan feel that greed is the only way to protect themselves from the horrors of war, these same circumstances of hardship inspire Anne to feel even more generous.

THEMES

MOTIFS

Motifs are recurring structures, contrasts, or literary devices that can help to develop and inform the text's major themes.

BECOMING A WOMAN
Anne is thirteen years old when she first goes into hiding in the annex, and she turns fifteen shortly before the family's arrest. Thus, her diary is a powerful firsthand record of the experience of a young girl as she matures. Although Anne faces the challenges of puberty under unusual circumstances, the issues she struggles with are universal. She frequently contemplates the changes in her body and her psychology. Because Anne does not readily confide in her mother or her sister, she turns to her diary to understand the changes she perceives and to question issues about sexuality and maturity. In later entries, as Anne begins to see herself as an independent woman, she compares herself to her mother and to other women of her mother's generation, imagining what she will be like in the future. She often thinks about what it means to be a woman and a mother, typically using her mother as an example of the type of woman she does not want to become. Instead, Anne seeks to overcome the obstacles of gender bias and prejudice, just as she hopes to escape the persecution faced by the Jewish people.

FEAR
The Franks and the van Daans are fortunate enough to have made advance plans to go into hiding should the need arise, but they still know they are not completely safe from the Nazis. Their security depends on the cooperation of many different people outside the annex, as well as a good amount of luck and hope. Their fear grows each time the doorbell rings, there is a knock on their door, or they hear that there is a break-in at the office building. They hear reports from the outside world about their friends who are arrested and about non-Jews who are suffering from a lack of food. As the war rages on around them, all people—Jews and non-Jews—suffer. Anne knows that her family's situation is precarious, and she spends much of her time trying to distract herself from this frightening reality. However, each scare does color her diary entries. She knows what would happen to her and her family if they were discovered, and this fear that permeates life in the annex likewise permeates the tone of Anne's diary.

SYMBOLS

Symbols are objects, characters, figures, or colors used to represent abstract ideas or concepts.

HANNELI

Hanneli is one of Anne's close friends who appears in Anne's dreams several times as a symbol of guilt. Hanneli appears sad and dressed in rags, and she wishes that Anne could stop Hanneli's suffering. A young Jewish girl, Hanneli has presumably already been arrested and deported to a concentration camp. For Anne, Hanneli represents the fate of her friends and companions and the millions of Jews—many of whom were children like herself—who were tortured and murdered by the Nazis. Anne questions why her friend has to suffer while she survives in hiding. Anne continually struggles with the guilt that her friend is dead while she is still alive. Hanneli's appearance in Anne's dreams makes Anne turn to God for answers and comfort, since there is no one else who can explain why she lives while her friend does not.

ANNE'S GRANDMOTHER

Anne's grandmother appears to Anne in her dreams. To Anne, she symbolizes unconditional love and support, as well as regret and nostalgia for the life Anne lived before being forced into hiding. Anne wishes she could tell her grandmother how much they all love her, just as she wishes she had appreciated her own life before she was confined in the annex. Anne misses living a life in which she did not have to worry about her future. She imagines that her grandmother is her guardian angel and will protect her, and she returns to this image to sustain her when she feels particularly afraid or insecure.

Summary & Analysis

JUNE 12, 1942–JUNE 24, 1942

SUMMARY

> *I hope I will be able to confide everything to you, as I have never been able to confide in anyone, and I hope you will be a great source of comfort and support.*
> (See QUOTATIONS, p. 45)

Anne Frank begins her diary with the hope that she will be able to reveal everything to it, since she feels that she has never truly been able to confide in anyone. She tells the story of how she acquired the diary on Friday, June 12, her thirteenth birthday. Anne wakes up at six in the morning and waits until seven to open her presents. One of the presents is the new diary. Afterward, Anne's friend Hanneli picks her up for school. Anne goes to gym with the other students, although she is not able to participate because her shoulders and hips dislocate too easily. She returns home at five in the afternoon. She describes several of her friends—Hanneli, Sanne, and Jacqueline—whom she has met at the Jewish Lyceum, the local school for Jewish children.

Anne writes about her birthday party on Sunday and continues to describe her classmates. She believes that "paper is more patient than people" and feels that she does not have any true friends and confidants. She has a loving family and many people she could call friends or admirers, but she cannot confide in any of them.

Anne then provides a brief overview of her childhood. She was born in Frankfurt, Germany, in 1929. Her family moved to Holland in 1933 because they were Jewish and her father found a job at a Dutch chemical company. Anne went to a Montessori nursery school and then went on to the Jewish Lyceum.

Anne says that her family's lives are somewhat anxious, especially since they have relatives still living in Germany. Her two uncles fled to North America, and her grandmother came to Holland to live with Anne's family. After 1940, the Nazis occupied Holland and instituted restrictive laws forcing Jews to wear yellow stars to identify themselves. The Germans forced the Jews to turn in their bicycles and shop only during certain hours. Jews were also restricted from riding streetcars, going outside at night, visiting Christian homes, and attending most schools. Anne's grandmother died in 1942, in the midst of this difficult time.

Anne starts addressing her diary as "Kitty" and writes that she and her friends have started a Ping-Pong club. After playing Ping-Pong, the girls go to the nearest ice cream shop that permits Jews, and they let admirers buy them ice cream. Anne complains that she knows boys will become enamored with her right away when she lets them bicycle home with her, so she tries to ignore them. Anne tells Kitty that her entire class is "quaking in their boots" and waiting to hear who will be promoted to the next grade. She is not worried about any subject except math, because in math class she was punished for talking too much. Anne adds that after she wrote a few funny essays on her punishment, the teacher began joking along with her.

Anne notes that it is hot and realizes what a luxury it is to ride in a streetcar, since Jews cannot use them anymore. The ferryman lets them ride the ferry, and Anne says that it is not the fault of the Dutch that the Jews are being persecuted. She tells her diary that a boy, Hello Silberberg, approached her and that they have started to see each other more often.

ANALYSIS

Despite the ominous circumstances for Jews in the Netherlands, Anne's interests are typical for a thirteen-year-old girl from a stable, middle-class family. She mentions the Jewish Lyceum casually, not dwelling on the laws that prevent Jews from attending other schools. Her carefree tone of voice and the topics she explores, such as friendship and gym class, show that she and many other Jews have adapted to their adverse situation without focusing on the difficulties or fears that they face.

Anne's worries about not having enough friends and not getting along well with her mother show that she is a typical adolescent, even in the face of danger. She does not think too much about the war or about her fear of being arrested by the Gestapo. Instead, she focuses on the details of what is happening at school and in her family. When she begins a diary entry with "our entire class is quaking in its boots," we immediately assume that something drastic has occurred because of the Germans and that everyone in the class is afraid. However, Anne is just referring to a mundane school matter. Her diary entries suggest that she is living her life from moment to moment and is deeply enmeshed in her social and educational world.

Anne's diary entries tell us much about her character. From the very beginning, we see that Anne is confident, thoughtful, and creative. She is also a very detailed observer, as evidenced by her lists of birthday presents and her meticulous descriptions of her friends. Anne also seems very disciplined, since she writes lengthy diary entries quite often. Anne's diligence in writing seems to help her release strong feelings instead of blurting them out loud and hurting her family and friends. When Anne remarks that paper is more patient than people, she emphasizes the difficulty she has expressing herself openly in front of others. We assume that she is afraid to confide in people because she is scared that she will hurt her friends and family. Thus, Anne shows us that although she is critical of others' faults, she is sensitive to their feelings.

Anne's candor led her father to omit certain sections of her diary when it was first published. He felt that certain passages were unflattering toward some of the annex's residents, most of whom died in the war. Indeed, in the diary, Anne is always very honest about her feelings and opinions and often insults others. Later, we learn that the others often do not tolerate Anne's frankness. Later editions of Anne's diary include some of the entries that Mr. Frank originally omitted. The inclusion of these passages, whether complimentary or disparaging, help us better understand Anne's development as a woman and her relationships with her friends and family members.

Anne's diary gives her the freedom to express her views however she wishes. When reading Anne's entries, we realize that they show her perspective alone. The entries are, of course, subjective, colored by Anne's views and not necessarily portraying the entire story of a person or an event. In later entries, Anne generally takes back any previous insults she wrote earlier in the heat of the moment. Thus, despite her stubborn nature and quick temper, Anne demonstrates that she is kind, fair, and forgiving at heart.

In contrast to later entries, Anne's early writings hardly mention her family members. Anne briefly introduces her family, but until they go into hiding, they do not seem to play a large role in Anne's daily thoughts. She refers to her mother and father as "loving parents," and from her brief descriptions they seem caring and easygoing. Anne does not mention the difficulties she has with her mother, which become a frequent subject in later entries. Anne's lack of detail about her family suggests that she has so much going on in her own life that she does not need to dwell on family relationships. When her father, mother, and sister do appear in these first entries, it is usually because Anne observed them doing something peripheral to her story, not because she is thinking about her relationship with them. The family's imminent confinement drastically changes the way Anne thinks about her relation to her family.

JULY 1, 1942–JULY 10, 1942

SUMMARY

Anne tells her diary that she has been seeing more of Hello. Hello's parents are in Belgium, but there is no way for him to travel there, so he is living in Amsterdam with his grandparents. On Sunday afternoon, Hello tells Anne that his grandmother did not approve of his association with such a young girl. He also says that he prefers Anne to his old girlfriend Ursul. Hello tells Anne that he will be free Wednesday evenings as well as parts of Saturdays and Sundays, since he used to go to meetings for a Zionist organization but decided not to attend them anymore. On Monday, he meets Anne's parents, then he and Anne go for a walk and do not return until after eight in the evening. Anne's father is furious, and she promises to return before eight in the future. Anne confesses that she is really in love with a boy named Peter, even though he is dating other girls, and that Hello is just a friend or a beau.

Anne receives decent grades on her report card but adds that her parents do not care about grades as much as some of her friends' parents do. Anne's father explains that they will likely have to go into hiding soon, which is why they have been asking friends to store their belongings. He tells her that they will "leave of [their] own accord" instead of waiting for the Germans to take them and that Anne does not have to worry about it right away. She is greatly dismayed by her father's plans. Three days later, on Sunday afternoon, Anne's sister, Margot, tells her that their father had received a call-up notice from the SS, the elite Nazi guard. Later, alone in their room, Margot tells Anne that it was really herself, not Mr. Frank, who had been called up. The girls quickly start packing their things. The next day, they pile on as many layers of clothes as they can, since they cannot risk carrying suitcases. Margot leaves the house first, carrying a schoolbag full of books, and Anne follows later that evening.

Eventually, the entire family arrives at their hiding place in Otto Frank's office building at 263 Prinsengracht. A secret annex was hidden upstairs from the office, behind a big gray door. Four people who work in the office are informed of the Franks' arrival. Margot is waiting for the rest of the family in the annex, which is stocked with dozens of cardboard boxes that had been sent over time. Anne and her father start unpacking the boxes as her mother and sister sleep. Anne writes that she did not have time until Wednesday to consider the "enormous change in [her] life," and that she finally had time to tell her diary about it and think about "what had happened to [her] and what was yet to happen."

ANALYSIS

This section illustrates the poignant contrast between Anne's innocence and the gravity of her family's situation. Having lived a fairly sheltered life thus far in Amsterdam, Anne is naturally focused on normal concerns such as grades and her relationships with boys. Anne writes in detail about her experiences with Hello, which appear to be the most important aspect of her life. Like a typical teenager, Anne focuses on the little nuances of her relationships, experiencing emotional ups and downs based on the type of attention she receives from boys and her friends. However, the events that force the Franks into hiding trivialize every subject that Anne has written about so far. The new gravity of her situation forces Anne to grow up quickly and understand issues that are much bigger than her small social world.

Anne's writing style changes with the transition to her new life in the annex. When the family is forced into hiding, Anne's writing becomes more terse. As the family makes preparations to leave their home, Anne writes, "After that it was quiet in our apartment; none of us felt like eating. It was still hot, and everything was very strange." Anne seems to find comfort in making such concise observations. She makes sure to document each moment of the frightening night when the Franks realize they must hide. When her family is feeling tense and fearful, Anne turns to her diary for comfort so that she does not have to depend on the already worried adults. This shows Anne's considerable independence for her young age. She knows that a serious upheaval is occurring in her family's life, but she does not panic or cry to her drained parents. Anne instead relies on her journal to support her and drowns out her fears with numerous peripheral details, such as the intricate layout of the annex and the family's moment-by-moment actions. She likewise seems to take comfort in busying herself with practical tasks, as she and Mr. Frank unpack the family's boxes while the others sleep.

Anne has always been aware of prejudice against Jews and of the dangers created by the war. At the same time, she has not felt a sense of immediate danger, so her concerns are focused on mundane issues of daily life. When her family is forced to hide, Anne is confronted with a new reality and finds that she must reconsider the world and her relationship with it. She is particularly horrified that it is Margot, not Mr. Frank, who is called up by the SS. She realizes that the Nazi police do not give any special treatment to children or adults and that all Jews are equally at risk. Anne begins to learn that she can no longer live in the innocent social world of a young teenager and must suddenly confront the adult world and the harshness and dangers of the war.

JULY 11, 1942–OCTOBER 9, 1942

SUMMARY

Margot and Mr. and Mrs. Frank cannot get used to the chiming of the clock in the annex, but Anne feels reassured by it. She tells her diary that living in the annex is similar to being on vacation in a strange boarding house, and she thinks that the annex is probably the most comfortable hiding place in all of Holland. Anne's father had brought her movie posters to the attic in advance, so she plasters her bedroom walls with them. Anne looks forward to the arrival of the van Daans, the other family who will live with them in the annex. In a comment added to this section several months later, however, Anne expresses how upset she is about not being able to go outside and that she is terrified that they will be discovered and shot.

Anne begins to argue with her mother more frequently. She feels that she does not fit in with her mother or sister, who are both very sentimental. Anne thinks that her father is the only one who understands her. She knows that she will not be able to leave the annex until after the war and that only a few people will be able to visit them. However, she is still hopeful and dreams of many things.

The van Daan family arrives on July 13, 1942. They come one day ahead of schedule because German call-up notices are being sent out with increasing frequency and causing unrest. Mr. van Daan explains what happened after the Franks' disappearance. The Franks had deliberately spread false rumors to throw the Gestapo off their trail, so most of their friends think they went to Switzerland.

Mr. Voskuijl, the father of one of Mr. Frank's coworkers, builds a bookcase in front of the door to the annex to conceal it. Anne's mother and Mrs. van Daan argue a lot, and Peter van Daan annoys the Franks with his hypochondria. Anne adds that Mrs. van Daan and her mother both speak abominable Dutch but that she will properly transcribe it in her diary. Anne is also studying French and memorizes five irregular verbs each day. She complains that Mrs. van Daan criticizes her even though Anne is not her daughter.

Anne and the others in the annex must take turns using the hot water to take baths, and when the plumber visits the building, they must sit completely still. Every time the doorbell rings, Anne is terrified because she thinks it is the Gestapo. Later, Anne imagines that she is in Switzerland and has 150 guilders to spend. She hears only bad news about the fates of the Franks' many Jewish friends and begins to tackle the issue of her identity, since she is both a German and a Jew.

ANALYSIS

At first, Anne sees her new life in hiding as an adventure of sorts. Though the two families live in constant fear of capture, they spend their time thinking about simpler, more immediate problems. They often try to think of ways to escape boredom. Because they are in such close quarters, the residents begin to get annoyed with one another's quirks. Peter is a hypochondriac, Mrs. van Daan is critical, and Anne's mother and Peter's mother fight a lot and speak improper Dutch. At first Anne focuses on figuring out ways to avoid getting frustrated with the others or ways to stay quiet while the plumber is visiting. Anne's initial pleasure with the novelty of the annex quickly fades, as she becomes restless and frustrated at her inability to go outside or even open the curtains during daylight hours. Even Anne's pervasive optimism cannot keep her from feeling dread each time the doorbell rings. The mundane routines of daily life are not quite able to mask the constant ring of terror and fear in the annex.

The war causes Anne to struggle with her identity as both a German and a Jew. She initially identifies herself with the Germans, writing, "Fine specimens of humanity . . . and to think I'm actually one of them!" However, she immediately refutes her own statement, writing "No, that's not true, Hitler took away our nationality long ago. And besides, there are no greater enemies on earth than the Germans and the Jews." Anne's words demonstrate her contempt for the Nazis and her confusion at the fact that they are in fact fellow Germans. Anne feels a stronger connection to the Dutch, but her first instinct is to identify herself as German. She quickly rethinks this notion, realizing that the Nazis no longer consider Jews to be Germans.

The adults in the annex likely share Anne's confusion about their national and ethnic identity. Having lived in Germany for most of their lives, the Frank and the Van Daan adults have significant roots there. Thirty years earlier, Anne's father and other German Jews had fought for the German army in World War I. Likewise, in the Netherlands, Dutch Jews and non-Jews lived side by side, considering themselves members of a unified and integrated community. However, the Nazi regime's rise to power brought the painful realization that both Nazis and many other German people considered Jews foreign or different. As we see in Anne's identity crisis, the Nazi regime killed not only Jewish people but also the Jewish community's collective connection to its past. While the Nazis forced Jews to wear stars to mark their identity, they simultaneous stripped the Jews of their identity as members of society.

Anne's diary demonstrates the impact the Holocaust has on a single girl, which personalizes this sprawling historical horror. Anne becomes preoccupied with questions about who she is and whom she wants to become, and her once innocent perspective changes considerably. The Holocaust forces Anne to grow up and come to terms with her own identity—her role as a member of her family, as a Jew, and as a young woman in a dangerous, threatening world.

OCTOBER 14, 1942–
NOVEMBER 20, 1942

SUMMARY
Anne continues to keep busy by studying French, math, history, and shorthand. She writes that she is getting along with her

mother and Margot better. The two sisters agree to let each other read their diaries. Anne asks Margot what she wants to be when she grows up, but Margot is mysterious about it.

Anne and the others in the annex have a scare when a carpenter comes to fill the fire extinguishers without advanced warning. They hear someone banging on the bookcase and they think the carpenter is going to discover them, but then they realize it is Mr. Kleiman, a man who helped them hide, trying to move the door since it is stuck. Miep Gies, a worker in Mr. Frank's office, spends a night in the annex along with her husband, Jan. Anne enjoys having the visitors around.

Later in the week, Mr. Frank becomes ill, but the family cannot call a doctor. That weekend, Bep Voskuijl, another worker in Mr. Frank's office, stays in the annex. Anne writes that she is very excited because she thinks she is about to get her period. In a note she adds to this section in 1944, Anne writes that she cannot believe her "childish innocence" from that time, and she calls her descriptions "indelicate." She also mentions how the whole time she has been in hiding she has longed for "trust, love and physical affection."

Anne reports on some of the British successes in Africa and puzzles over Churchill's famous quotation about the war being at "the end of the beginning." Mr. Frank recovers from his illness, and Peter turns sixteen. The residents of the annex also agree to take in an eighth person, and Anne is very excited at the prospect of a new addition.

The newcomer is Albert Dussel, a dentist who is married to a Christian woman. Mr. Dussel is excited when Miep tells him of the hiding place, but he asks for a few extra days to put his accounts in order and treat some patients. Mr. Dussel meets Mr. Kleiman at an appointed time, and Miep then leads him to the annex. Mr. Dussel is surprised to see the Frank family because he had heard they were in Belgium.

The van Daans give Mr. Dussel a tongue-in-cheek list of rules upon his arrival. He shares a room with Anne and tells her about the atrocities committed outside, including the murders of women and children. Anne thinks that they are lucky to be in hiding, and she thinks of the suffering her friends must endure merely because they are Jewish. Anne writes that she is very upset by the news, but she resolves that she cannot spend all her time crying. The loneliness of the attic makes her unhappy.

ANALYSIS

In this section we see Anne's strength in the face of mounting fears. Anne begins to worry more about an intrusion into the annex, but nonetheless continues to detail the day-to-day changes in her emotions and passes the time with her studies. For the first time, Anne writes about feeling closer to Margot, but we do not get a good idea of Margot's character. Margot does not share Anne's plans for the future, which suggests that she is afraid she will not have a future at all.

Anne does not make any overt attempt to get to know the other members of the annex, except for Peter. This may seem odd considering the confined nature of the annex. However, social and familial structures of the 1940s were often formal and inhibited personal intimacy between generations or with people outside the family. In addition, since Anne is going through puberty, she is understandably more focused on what is going on in her own life and does not necessarily have a strong enough sense of self to engage deeply with the adults. Furthermore, the group's stressful living conditions put everyone on edge, making them less inclined to open up in a meaningful way. Many of the residents seem to guard their inner thoughts from even their close family members.

For Anne, the early excitement of being in hiding gives way to frustration at being trapped in such close quarters with the van Daans and her own family. Mr. Dussel's arrival is initially exciting for Anne because it brings a change in a life that has little variety. However, this sense of excitement is soured when Mr. Dussel tells Anne about the persecution of Jews in the outside world. Anne begins to express her inability to understand the injustice of persecution and genocide. For Anne, the probable deaths of her friends and acquaintances are still abstract in her mind and have not yet become real. She knows rationally what is happening outside of the annex, but the relative security of the hiding place allows her to escape the harsh realities of the war and retain some of her childhood innocence.

NOVEMBER 28, 1942–JUNE 13, 1943

SUMMARY

The residents of the annex use too much electricity and exceed their ration. Anne begins to feel that Mr. Dussel is a strict disciplinarian and has too many opinions about etiquette. She writes that it is very difficult being "the badly brought-up center of attention in a family of nitpickers." Hanukkah and St. Nicholas Day come on almost the same day, so the annex holds two celebrations. They light the Hanukkah candles for only ten minutes, since candles are in short supply. For St. Nicholas Day, Father hides a basket filled with presents and a mask of Black Peter in a cabinet.

Mr. van Daan makes sausages to preserve the meat they have bought. Mr. Dussel opens a pretend dental practice in the annex and comically attempts to fix Mrs. van Daan's cavities. Anne tires of Mrs. van Daan's incessant complaints and is annoyed that Mr. Dussel constantly tells her to be quiet at night but then wakes her up when he does his exercises at dawn. Anne marvels at how diplomatic she has become while living in the annex. Mr. Kugler brings the residents gravy packets to fill because he can find no one else to do the job. According to Anne, however, it is a prisoner's job.

Anne writes more about the terrible events that are happening outside. Jews are being taken from their homes and separated from their families, and non-Jewish children are wandering the streets in hunger. Anne writes that both Christians and Jews want the war to end, and she believes that her family is better off than people outside the annex.

Anne seethes that everyone is always yelling at her and calling her "exasperating," and she wishes she had a personality that did not antagonize everyone. Mr. Frank thinks the war will end soon, but the level of anxiety in the annex increases. Anne is frightened by the sound of gunfire one night, so she crawls into her father's bed for comfort. Another night, Peter climbs up into the loft and a rat bites his arm. Mr. Dussel often writes letters to his wife and to others outside, and Mr. Frank demands that he stop. The residents have another scare when they think they hear burglars in the building. After that incident, the clock suddenly stops chiming, which also upsets Anne. Later, the residents hear a radio announcement that all Jews must be deported from Utrecht and the other provinces of the Netherlands by the beginning of July.

Mr. Dussel's wife sends him a package for his birthday. Anne notes that Mr. Dussel does not share his sizable stash of personal food with the other residents or their Dutch helpers. Although Anne knows that her family is better off than the vast majority of Jews, she predicts that they will look back and wonder how they lived for so long under such difficult conditions. Mr. van Daan says he believes that the war will end in 1943. When Anne reaches her fourteenth birthday, her father writes her a poem, and Margot translates it from German into Dutch.

ANALYSIS

In this section Anne vents her frustrations at living in the annex and dealing with the adults. Anne realizes that the general unpleasantness of the annex and the van Daans' and Mr. Dussel's stinginess pale in comparison to the horrors others are enduring outside the annex. Nonetheless, Anne is frustrated at the adults and does not think their behavior is warranted. She does not seem to make much effort to understand why the adults are acting the way they are. This oversight reminds us that although Anne has grown up considerably since moving into the annex, she is a young girl and still emotionally immature in certain ways. She never takes a step back to try to understand the different pressures facing the adults. At her age, she is still struggling to understand her own nature and motivations, and she is not yet able to expand her focus to include the adults and their behavior. Reading her diary, we realize that Anne does not bear the burden of trying to protect an entire family from the inexplicable evils of the war. On the one hand, Anne has the perspective to realize that her situation within the annex is not as dire as the situation outside; however, she does not yet have the empathy to understand the cause of the adults' tensions.

The Franks' holiday observances suggest that even during terrible times, they still want to celebrate life. Hanukkah brings them some joy, though they must ration their use of Hanukkah candles because supplies are scarce. St. Nicholas Day is a traditional Dutch holiday that marks the advent of Christmas, and Black Peter is the companion to Father Christmas, or Santa Claus. The fact that the Franks celebrate Jewish and Christian holidays, and that Anne believes that both the Christians and Jews want the war to end, reflects the family's assimilation into European culture. Their acceptance of other cultures and religions makes it even more difficult for the Franks to comprehend the persecution of the Jews and their treatment as outsiders.

Anne increasingly interrupts her descriptions of the minutiae and social dynamics of the annex with comparisons between the annex and the world outside. The radio keeps the residents informed of the latest atrocities being committed outside their door, and the break-ins disturb their already precarious sense of safety. Anne alternately feels that living in hiding is saving her life and that it unfairly condemns her. Working out her thoughts in the diary helps Anne make sense of the new world and the inconceivable reality she is forced to inhabit. She begins to see herself as a young girl trapped in a conflict that does not involve her directly. Anne looks to the future and the end of the war, imagining that the persecution of her people will end and she will be free again.

JUNE 15, 1943–NOVEMBER 11, 1943

SUMMARY

> *I can only cry out and implore, "Oh ring, ring, open wide and let us out!"*
> (See QUOTATIONS, p. 46)

Mr. Voskuijl is diagnosed with cancer and knows he does not have long to live. Anne decides to stop studying shorthand because she is becoming nearsighted and cannot get glasses. The group briefly considers sending her out to an ophthalmologist, but Mr. Frank has heard that the British have landed in Sicily, Italy, and thinks the war will soon be over. Anne's favorite day of the week is Saturday, when Bep brings books from the library. Anne asks Mr. Dussel if she can use the table in their room to study during the afternoon, but he refuses. They argue over it, so Mr. Frank intervenes and arranges for Anne to have access to the table for two afternoons each week. There is another break-in at the office, and this time the robbers take cash and ration coupons for sugar. Anne writes about what she plans to do when they are able to leave the annex. She says she would be so overjoyed she would not know where to start, but she wants to go back to school again.

Two air-raid sirens sound in one day as bombs fall relentlessly on Amsterdam. The residents of the annex are scared, but Anne tries to be brave. On the radio they hear the good news that

Benito Mussolini, Italy's Fascist leader, has been deposed. They are forced to turn in the radio, which angers Mr. Dussel. Anne describes the complicated daily schedule of the annex, pointing out that it is very different from the routine that ordinary people would follow during ordinary times. Her account, as usual, is filled with humorous and not very complimentary descriptions of the other people in the annex.

Anne receives new shoes, and Mr. Dussel almost causes trouble by asking Miep to bring him a banned book. Italy surrenders unconditionally, but Anne's happiness is tempered by the news that Mr. Kleiman will have to undergo a serious stomach operation. She also worries that Mr. van Maaren, a man who works in the warehouse and is not trustworthy, will find out about the hiding place. Anne writes that she has been taking medication every day for depression. Bep is exasperated with the number of errands they ask her to run, and everyone's temper is constantly flaring up. Anne compares herself to a bird with broken wings, longing for fresh air and sunshine.

Margot decides to take a correspondence course in Latin to ease her boredom, but Anne says it is too difficult. Mr. Frank asks Mr. Kleiman for a children's Bible so that Anne can learn about the New Testament. Miep tells Anne that she envies the peace and quiet of the annex. But Anne, who is constantly afraid of being discovered, compares the eight residents to a patch of blue sky surrounded by dark clouds. The clouds are coming in, and they can see both the destruction below them and the peace above them.

Anne writes a memorial to her fountain pen, which she has owned for many years but which was accidentally melted in the stove. She says that her only consolation is that the pen was cremated, as she hopes to be when she dies.

Analysis

By the middle of 1943, Anne's mood becomes darker as her frustration and anger increase. She has plenty of time to contemplate the war, and in each diary entry her anxiety grows. Her tone is less cheerful and humorous, despite occasional injections of satire or sarcasm, particularly when she is annoyed with another resident of the annex. While Anne tries to act like a brave adult, she still jumps into her father's bed during air raids and takes medication for her depression. Anne is still just a young girl and can no longer pretend to be strong.

Anne gives a cynical description of her discovery that hypocrisy rather than honesty is the only way to get along with people. She displays her newfound skill at hypocrisy in her negotiations with Mr. Dussel over the study table in their bedroom. Although she considers Mr. Dussel rude and impossible to deal with, she swallows her feelings to gain the upper hand. By maintaining her composure, Anne feels superior to the "petty and pedantic" Dussel. Her language and behavior show us that the once-lighthearted girl is becoming depressed and cynical, trusting less in the security of her parents and relying more on her own resourcefulness.

Although the Franks are being persecuted as Jews, they clearly see themselves as part of society as a whole, not members of a separate group. Mr. Frank demonstrates his open-mindedness when he decides to buy Anne a Bible. Additionally, since the Franks and the van Daans do not keep kosher but do celebrate both Jewish and Christian holidays, they most likely identified themselves as Germans first and Jews second. Their identity became unclear when Hitler came to power and they lost their German citizenship. Despite the forced segregation imposed in the Netherlands, the Franks settled in comfortably enough for Anne to consider herself part of wider Dutch society.

In this section, Anne also describes more of Miep's role in keeping the annex running and gives us a sense of the amount of work Miep has to do to keep them supplied in secret. Anne understands Miep's envy of the people in the annex, since the situation outside is not favorable for any of the Dutch people, even non-Jews. The people who protect the annex are under just as much stress as those inside. Nonetheless, Anne knows that Miep is unaware of the difficulties of their life in hiding, such as the constant quarreling and frustration at being in such close quarters. Miep does not understand what it is like to be a young girl, trapped in a small attic with a whole world just out of reach.

Anne's language becomes more metaphorical in this part of the diary, as she increasingly attempts to describe her fear and depression using figurative language. She chooses to describe her situation in terms of the natural environment, the part of the world she misses most while she is in hiding. She compares herself to a bird with a broken wing and compares the eight residents to clouds caught between peace and war. Anne uses these comparisons to nature to express her feelings and desires that are too difficult to describe in literal terms.

SUMMARY & ANALYSIS

NOVEMBER 17, 1943–
JANUARY 28, 1944

SUMMARY

> *I sometimes wonder if anyone will ever . . . overlook*
> *my ingratitude and not worry about whether or not*
> *I'm Jewish and merely see me as a teenager badly in*
> *need of some good, plain fun.*
>
> (See QUOTATIONS, p. 47)

Bep is forced to stay away from the annex for six weeks because of
an outbreak of diphtheria at her house. Margot continues the Latin
correspondence course using Bep's name. Mr. Dussel fights with
Mrs. van Daan, who thinks he and the rest of the annex should go to
dinner in honor of his first anniversary of living there. Anne notes
that Mr. Dussel has not once thanked them for taking him into the
annex. At night, she dreams that she sees Hanneli, who asks Anne to
rescue her. Anne regrets not treating Hanneli better and feels guilty
that she is still relatively safe while Hanneli is suffering.

St. Nicholas Day comes again, and Anne decorates a laundry
basket with colorful paper and fills it with shoes. She and her father
write verses and put one in each shoe. Anne comes down with the flu
and receives an assortment of supposed remedies. Everyone
exchanges Christmas and Hanukkah presents, but spirits are low
because the war is at an impasse. Anne is still grateful that her situation is better than that of other Jewish children, but she cannot help
feeling jealous of Mrs. Kleiman's children. Her children can go outside and play with friends, while Anne's family and friends are
trapped in the annex like "lepers."

Anne dreams about Hanneli again and also about her own
grandmother. She wonders whether Hanneli is still alive. Later,
Anne reads through her diary and is shocked at how negatively she
wrote of her mother in past entries. Anne thinks she has grown wiser
since then and now understands her mother better. She sees herself
as an adolescent now and says that when she is having her period
she feels like she has a "sweet secret." Anne also mentions the
ecstasy she feels at seeing a female nude, such as the Venus de Milo
statue, and she talks about how she once had a "terrible desire" to
kiss a female friend. Now that she has no female friends, she is so
desperate for someone to talk to that she begins to confide in Peter

van Daan. Anne also dreams about Peter Schiff, an older friend on whom she had a long crush. She tells the story of their relationship and says that she does not need a photograph of Peter because his face is still clear in her mind.

Anne and Peter talk about a cat, Boche. Peter says that Boche is a tomcat and turns the cat over to show Anne his genitalia. Anne says that she knows the female sexual organ is called the vagina, but she does not know what the male sexual organ is called. Peter says he will ask his parents. Anne is impressed that Peter can discuss such things without any shame.

ANALYSIS

Anne's dreams in this section demonstrate how deeply the war haunts her. The fears, loneliness, and insecurities that she feels uncomfortable expressing out loud emerge in her dreams about Hanneli and her grandmother. Anne assumes that Hanneli has been deported to the concentration camps. She knows that she is powerless to save her friends, yet she feels guilty that they are suffering and she is not. Despite acknowledging her relatively good fortune thus far, Anne is envious of the non-Jewish children in Amsterdam who can still play and move about freely.

The appearance of Anne's grandmother in her dream emphasizes Anne's longing for security. Anne imagines that her grandmother is her guardian angel and will protect her. She attempts to find comfort from the stability of previous generations embodied in the protective, maternal figure of her grandmother. Anne's dreams reflect the profound feelings of sadness and loneliness that she feels she must put aside for the good of the group. Anne acknowledges the reality of their situation and realizes that if they all succumbed to their feelings of anxiety and depression, living in the annex would become unbearable.

As Anne goes through puberty, we see her becoming more mature, thoughtful, and more aware of her body. Her confinement forces her to struggle with many of the questions of adolescence by herself, since there are no other girls her age with whom she could share her experiences. Thus, the diary becomes an important tool for Anne's self-discovery and maturity. She starts to feel disconnected from "the Anne of last year" as she looks over past diary entries about her mother, which she now considers the product of her immaturity and girlish moods. Anne has a record of all of her private yet indignant temper tantrums, which allows her to see how much she has changed in such a short time. Writing in the diary allows Anne to express her unkind and indulgent emotions and explore her own personal desires in a way that will not hurt anyone else. Anne's candor caused Otto Frank to cut many parts of the diary in its original publication. Anne's judgments, though at times cruel, are an important aspect of her personality and her experiences. Anne's written outbursts provide a full sense of who she is and how she changes while she is in the annex.

With her diary as her only confidant, Anne misses both her female and male friends, and she thinks often of her love, Peter Schiff. She is drawn to Peter van Daan, since he is the only young man sharing her experience. Anne is naturally curious about Peter because he is a teenage male, and as a girl in puberty, she is fascinated by his body. Anne's discussion of the cat's genitalia represents an important moment for her, since it allows her to confront sexuality openly and with a male for the first time. Without female friends to discuss her innermost secrets, Anne learns about herself the only way she can, through introspection and through interactions with her limited environment.

JANUARY 28, 1944 (EVENING)– MARCH 11, 1944

SUMMARY

Anne writes that she is growing more bored in the annex and tires of listening to the same stories over and over again. The adults constantly repeat the stories they have heard from Mr. Kleiman, Jan, and Miep, which are mainly stories about other Jews who are in hiding. Anne is very impressed by the Dutch people who are helping Jews hide, since they are risking their own lives in an attempt to save others. She goes downstairs one night and feels that she cannot count on anyone else to support her. However, Anne's fears vanish as she looks up into the sky and puts her faith in God. She has an intense desire to be alone, but she worries that someday she will be more alone than she would like.

Anne's personal life has changed considerably since the weekend, when she noticed Peter looking at her "not in the usual way." The next day, Peter confides that he is often too nervous to speak to people and that he used to beat up people instead of talking to them.

Anne is happy to learn that Peter is also temperamental. On Margot's birthday, Anne and Peter talk again, and Peter says he is sure Britain will go to war against Russia. Peter also adds that he is sorry he was born a Jew. Anne is disappointed to find out that although Peter does not want to be Christian, he wants to make sure no one knows he is Jewish after the war. He says that the Jews are the chosen people, and Anne exclaims, "Just this once, I hope they'll be chosen for something good!"

Anne starts to enjoy going upstairs to see Peter, and she says her life is much better now that she has something to look forward to. However, she adds that she is not in love. All the same, Anne's mother does not like the idea of her going upstairs. A few days later, Anne writes that she thinks about Peter all the time and that Peter van Daan and Peter Schiff have melted into one Peter. Anne's newfound happiness is briefly shaken after another, more serious break-in at the office. It seems that the burglar has a duplicate key.

Anne writes about love, saying that emotional love eventually leads to physical love, and that she considers this a natural progression and does not worry about losing her "virtue." She imagines that her grandmother is watching over and protecting her. Mrs. van Daan teases Anne about Peter. In a particularly self-reflective entry, Anne thinks back on her life before coming to the annex. She says that her life was heavenly but that she was superficial and very different back then. Anne remarks that her carefree days as a schoolgirl are gone forever, but she does not miss them.

Anne also looks back over her time in the annex and distinguishes different periods in her growing maturity. In 1942, she said that the transition from a life "filled with sunshine" to one of quarrels and accusations made her stubborn and insolent. In 1943 she was sad, lonely and self-critical but then became a teenager and was treated more like a grown-up. She gained a deeper insight into her family and the other members of the annex, and she began to feel more emotionally independent. Now, in 1944, she has begun to discover her longing "not for a girlfriend, but for a boyfriend," and she has noticed a new depth to her emotions and sense of self. Anne also sadly notes that the police have arrested Mr. M., a man who had provided her family with food. The residents are scared anew when they hear a knock on the wall next door during dinner.

SUMMARY & ANALYSIS

ANALYSIS

By this point in her diary, Anne has gained a fuller sense of self and a clearer view of her relationships with the people in the annex. She starts signing her diary "Anne M. Frank" instead of simply "Anne," a sign that she perceives her own coming of age. Anne has matured significantly during her time in the annex, particularly because her family's time in hiding coincided with Anne's puberty. In this confined world, Anne has also developed her relationships with her family, because the close quarters have forced her to understand her parents and sister on a deeper level.

Confinement in the annex has changed Peter as well. He opens up to Anne emotionally, whereas he previously used physical force instead of connecting with other people. Anne finds in Peter the confidant for whom she had been longing. She becomes aware of her feelings for the opposite sex, a new aspect of maturity and development as a young woman that changes her entire experience of living in the annex.

With life in the annex becoming more tedious and oppressive, Peter's empathy and companionship provide Anne with significant emotional and mental relief. Since her physical life is so static and confined, Anne instead begins to look forward to emotional changes such as the development of her feelings for Peter. Because of the physical confinement of the annex, the evolution of Peter and Anne's relationship is on display for everyone else to see. As Peter becomes an object of desire for Anne, the adults begin to comment on the appropriateness of the relationship, and Mrs. van Daan constantly teases Anne. The lack of privacy forces Anne to confront issues with her family and sexuality long before she would have under normal circumstances.

Anne's growing maturity is also evident in the increased gravity of her discussions of her life and the war. For the first time, Anne writes seriously about the possibility of her own death, especially as her morale worsens. At the same time, she dreams about life after the war and about her great fortune in having a hiding place. She has become highly introspective and insightful about her own nature, and she begins to reflect on her past development and organize it into stages. Anne uses her diary like a literary timeline of her inner development, which she analyzes and critiques. By criticizing her own past actions and thoughts, she shows her capacity for personal growth and self-awareness, two important aspects of coming-of-age. Anne considers the possibility of her death, but she does not fully come to terms with the fact that the future may not come for her. Though maturing into a young woman, she still retains a measure of youthful innocence and idealism.

Anne and Peter also confront their identity as young Jews, a subject that Anne rarely touches upon in her diary. Anne does not consider the possibility of converting to Christianity and is shocked when Peter says that in the future he will hide the fact that he is Jewish. Anne is proud that she is Jewish and remains optimistic that the Jews will eventually be rewarded for their faith and not persecuted. Peter, however, is ashamed that he is Jewish and wants to separate himself from his past. The discussion that the two share and their different conclusions represent two common but opposite reactions to the Holocaust: a strengthening of Jewish identification versus a willful weakening of an association with Judaism.

MARCH 14, 1944–APRIL 11, 1944

SUMMARY

The people who supply food coupons to the annex are arrested. The residents' only alternative is the black-market ration books they have, and the food they must eat is horrible. Miep gets sick with the flu, and Jan says it is impossible to see a doctor. Anne says that she is more restless than Peter because he has his own room, while she has to share one with Mr. Dussel.

Anne and Margot are both growing annoyed with their parents. Anne complains that her parents are not open about sex and sexuality. She and Margot exchange letters. Margot writes that she is somewhat jealous of Anne's relationship with Peter, but only because she also wants someone with whom she can share her feelings. Anne is growing happier with her relationship with Peter but cannot fathom ever marrying him.

Anne decides to ask Peter about sex, since she believes "he knows everything," and later she talks to Margot in the bathroom. Peter overhears them and thinks Anne only spoke to him to tease him, but she tells him it is untrue. Anne says she would like to ask if Peter knows about female genitalia, and she writes a description of her own anatomy in her diary.

Anne's mother forbids Anne from going up to see Peter because Mrs. van Daan is jealous. Peter invites Margot to come upstairs with Anne. Listening to the radio at the end of March, Anne hears a mem-

SUMMARY & ANALYSIS

ber of the Dutch government in exile propose a collection of Dutch people's diaries and letters after the war. Anne writes that everyone in the annex immediately thought of her diary. She wonders what would happen if she published a novel about the annex, and thinks that ten years after the war people would find her diary very interesting. To pass the time, Anne continues writing stories and describes some of them in her diary. She also writes about her hobbies, such as genealogy and mythology. Food is growing scarce and there are no vegetables left.

Anne is talking to Peter one night when another break-in occurs. Mr. van Daan tries to scare the burglars away by shouting "Police!" but the residents see someone shine a flashlight through a gap in the wall and hear footsteps running away. Anne is terrified, thinking the Gestapo is about to come for them. The residents lie on the floor, petrified, and hear footsteps on the stairs and a rattling at the bookcase that hides the door to the annex. The noises stop but someone has left the light in front of the bookcase on.

Mrs. van Daan worries about the police finding the radio downstairs, and Otto Frank worries they will find Anne's diary. Anne writes, "If my diary goes, I go too." The adults phone Mr. Kleiman and wait in suspense until a knock comes on the door. They cry with relief when they see it is only Jan and Miep. Anne wonders why the Jews have been singled out for death. She decides that after the war she will become a Dutch citizen because she loves Holland and the Dutch. She writes, "If God lets me live . . . I'll make my voice heard."

ANALYSIS

As the danger increases, Anne's perspective about her future continues to mature. She continually shifts back and forth between feeling that she is about to die and making plans for her future. The closest encounter thus far with the police makes Anne contemplate death more seriously. The possibility of the family being discovered only increases with time, and the inhabitants take turns contemplating how they will behave when they are arrested. Anne begins to worry that she will not live to accomplish any of the things she hopes to, like writing a novel or pursuing her hobbies. However, she continues to think about her future and decides how she will identify herself after the war.

Although at the beginning of the diary she saw herself as a child, Anne is now beginning to discover her place in the world and see herself as an adult. In an early entry, on June 20, 1942, she had written, "It seems to me that later on neither I nor anyone else will be interested in the musings of a thirteen-year-old schoolgirl," because she did not think her thoughts were important for anyone except herself. Now, however, she is starting to become aware of the broader significance of her experience and realizes the potential value of sharing her words with others. With a newfound understanding of her own mortality, Anne recognizes the injustice of her fate more fully. She also realizes the value of her diary and her personal thoughts, and she expresses her hope that her diary will reach people after the war. Anne's written words about this hope are what convince her father to share the diary with others.

Otto Frank understandably chose to omit several passages from this section, including those concerning Anne's sexual curiosity. He believed that these were personal thoughts and were not necessarily suitable for a young-adult audience. These moments in which Anne expresses her sexuality are very important. We see Anne as a girl, rather than a sort of sterilized saint or victimized martyr. While Anne is a unique and remarkable individual with a tragic experience, we also see her as a normal girl, with typical human fears and desires. If Anne's diary entries focused only on the war or her hiding, we would feel less connected to her tragedy. However, Anne intersperses her thoughts about death and the war with accounts of time spent with Peter and her growing sexuality. We feel a greater connection and identification with Anne, and her tragedy causes even more emotional impact.

APRIL 14, 1944–AUGUST 1, 1944

SUMMARY

> [I] keep trying to find a way to become what I'd like to
> be and what I could be if . . . if only there were no
> other people in the world.   (See QUOTATIONS, p. 49)

Tensions in the annex run high after the break-in, and no one can shake the feeling of impending doom. On top of that, Peter forgets to unbolt the front door, so Mr. Kugler has to smash the window to get in. The air raids on the city are incredibly heavy. The Registry of Births, Deaths, and Marriages in The Hague is bombed, requiring new ration cards to be issued.

On April 15, 1944, Anne gets her first kiss. Although Peter only kisses her "half on [her] left cheek, half on [her] ear," Anne suddenly feels she is very advanced for her age. She writes that the longer the war drags on, the more difficulty she has imagining ever being liberated. Anne talks to Peter about female anatomy, which she has wanted him to do for a while. She then muses about trying to have a fairy-tale published in a magazine.

Anne writes about her schoolwork and also includes the family's war-ration recipe for potato kugel in her diary. She asks Peter if he thinks she should tell her father about their relationship, and he believes they should. Mr. Frank says that he thinks it is not a good idea to carry on a romance in the annex, and he asks Anne if Peter is in love with her. Mr. Frank tells her not to take it too seriously and that it is her responsibility to show restraint.

Anne wonders about the point of the war and laments that money is being spent on fighting rather than on medicine, the poor, and the arts. She reflects on human nature and concludes that until all of humanity undergoes a profound change, people's tendencies toward violence will lead to endless wars and destruction. Anne writes that she is "young and strong and living through a big adventure." Her father complains that she is going upstairs to see Peter too much. Anne wants to explain why she visits Peter a lot, so she writes her father a letter, which makes him very upset. He tells her it is the most hurtful letter he has ever received. Anne feels deeply ashamed and decides to try to improve herself.

Anne tells her diary the story of her family, including her parents' biographies. She writes that her wish is to become a famous journalist and writer. Mr. Frank has lost a bet with Mrs. van Daan about when the war will end, so he has to give her five jars of yogurt in payment. Anne hears that anti-Semitism is becoming more common among the Dutch, and she is deeply disheartened. She grows depressed again and wonders if it would not have been better to suffer a quick death rather than go into hiding. She counteracts this thought by writing that they all love life too much.

On June 6, 1944, D-Day, the BBC announces that the Allied invasion of France has begun. The residents of the annex are very excited. Anne turns fifteen and writes that the liberation is going "splendidly." Her mood improves, and she contemplates her love for nature and the question of why women are thought of as inferior to men. Near the end of July, Anne writes about an assassination attempt on Hitler and hopes it is proof that the Germans want to stop the war themselves. On August 1, 1944, Anne describes her new insights into her own character and muses that perhaps she could become the kind of person she wants to be "if only there were no other people in the world." Anne's diary ends abruptly.

ANALYSIS

> *It's difficult in times like these: ideals, dreams and cherished hopes rise within us, only to be crushed by grim reality.*
> (See QUOTATIONS, p. 48)

In this section we see a marked shift in Anne's writing, as she appears to be writing primarily for other readers rather than just for herself. She begins to think of herself as a writer and of her diary as a book. She also sees herself as more of an adult, though at times she is still writing from a child's perspective. Anne's final entries are a mixture of personal reflection, philosophical inquiry, humor, and complaints about her dissatisfaction with her family life and the way she is treated. In many ways, the end of the diary reads as a more self-conscious mixture of the ideas she presented earlier: a portrayal of an imaginative, ambitious teenager blended with evidence of the extraordinary and devastating circumstances of her life.

Though she maintains an optimistic innocence throughout, Anne clearly has matured over the time in which she keeps her diary. She becomes interested in love and sex, as can be seen in her feelings for Peter, and must reconcile those feelings with her desire to maintain a happy relationship with her father. But in addition to the normal psychological and physical changes associated with puberty and aging, Anne is deeply affected by the confinement, fear, guilt, anger, and sadness the war brings upon her. Faced with the life that has been forced upon her, Anne must enlarge her concept of the world and examine herself not only within the confines of her small family but in relation to a world that is demonstrating an implacable hatred of her. In her final entry, she begins to explore larger social issues, setting goals to become a successful woman and overcome obstacles she might encounter.

Although Anne clearly did not plan to end her diary where she did, it does serve as an appropriate ending to her account of her thoughts and experiences: a summation of her character and the struggles she has endured in trying to become the kind of person she imagines she can be. She takes a long, deep look at herself and is upset that people only know her public side. Anne is still afraid of sharing her more personal, sentimental inner self.

Anne's last sentence is a powerful statement, which is even stronger because it is the last we ever hear from her. She writes, "[W]hen everybody starts hovering over me, I get cross, then sad, and finally end up turning my heart inside out, the bad part on the outside and the good part on the inside, and keep trying to find a way to become what I'd like to be and what I could be if . . . if only there were no other people in the world." This passage conveys Anne's struggle with her inward and outward selves. Because she knows that there will always be both good and evil people in the world, she concludes that for only good to exist, there must be no other people at all. Anne realizes that she has tremendous potential but that it is stifled and contorted. Because of the evil that she faces—and that everyone in the world faces—no one can be exactly who he or she wants to be. Anne's words have an eerie prescience, since we know that she was killed at the hands of these "other people" just a few months after this last entry. Thus, the diary culminates with a precocious insight into human nature and a stinging poignancy.

Important Quotations Explained

1. I hope I will be able to confide everything to you, as I have never been able to confide in anyone, and I hope you will be a great source of comfort and support.

Anne writes this on the inside cover of her diary just after she receives it for her thirteenth birthday. At the time, she feels that she does not have any true confidants, which makes her feel lonely and misunderstood. Anne does, however, have many friends and admirers, and she is a playful, amusing, and social young girl. Thus, her sentiments in this passage may seem odd and a bit exaggerated, but she later explains that even though she has friends, she is never fully able to open up to them. Anne finds that she and her friends talk only about trivial things, even when she has deeper things on her mind that she wishes to share. For example, she never broaches the subjects of her developing body or Germany's occupation of Holland. Having a diary—which she addresses as "Kitty," like a friend—enables her to express her thoughts without fear of being criticized by others. Anne's relationship with her diary helps comfort her through her insecure, lonely, and fearful time in hiding.

2. I see the eight of us in the Annex as if we were a patch of blue sky surrounded by menacing black clouds. . . . [They loom] before us like an impenetrable wall, trying to crush us, but not yet able to. I can only cry out and implore, "Oh ring, ring, open wide and let us out!"

Anne records this vivid image on November 8, 1943, after living in the annex for more than a year. As the war rages on and people throughout Europe suffer, Anne is starting to become depressed and pessimistic about her family's chances of survival. She alternates between imagining what her future will be like and fearing that she and her family will be discovered at any time. Anne's writing becomes more metaphoric as she tries to express her fears and the anxiety and desperation that plague the residents of the annex. Nature is perhaps what Anne misses most about the outside world, so it follows that she describes her feeling of claustrophobia and entrapment with an image of nature. The image of blue sky suggests freedom. Dark clouds, signifying the oppression and restrictions on the Jews, cover the sky, suffocating Anne and the annex's other inhabitants. Anne's blue sky represents liberation. Both the sky and freedom remain beyond her reach.

3.   I sometimes wonder if anyone will ever understand
     what I mean, if anyone will ever overlook my
     ingratitude and not worry about whether or not I'm
     Jewish and merely see me as a teenager badly in need
     of some good, plain fun.

In this passage from December 24, 1943, Anne reminds us that she
is just a normal young girl who has been forced into extraordinary
circumstances. She willingly makes sacrifices and deals with the
restrictions of the annex without much complaint because she
knows that she is more fortunate than her friends who have already
been arrested and sent to concentration camps. This attitude demonstrates Anne's remarkable maturity, but it clearly takes its toll on
her spirit. Aside from wanting to return to the freedoms and com-
forts she had before the war, Anne simply wants to experience a
normal childhood. She does not want to live in a world that places
such significance on where she is from, what her religion is, or
whether she behaves well with adults. She wants to be in a place
where she does not have to worry whether she will live or whether
her friends are suffering. The diary has such emotional impact
because we see Anne not as a saint, but as a normal girl with real
human feelings and imperfections who falls victim to the tragedy of
the Holocaust.

4.   It's difficult in times like these: ideals, dreams and
      cherished hopes rise within us, only to be crushed by
      grim reality. It's a wonder I haven't abandoned all my
      ideals, they seem so absurd and impractical. Yet I
      cling to them because I still believe, in spite of
      everything, that people are truly good at heart.

Anne writes this on July 15, 1944, less than one month before the
Nazis arrest her and her family, sending them all to the concentration camps. This is perhaps the most well-known quotation from
Anne's diary because it is a brazen expression of optimism in the
face of imminent and incomprehensible cruelty. The passage also
provides a brief glimpse into Anne's mind during her last days in the
annex and demonstrates how much she has changed from when her
family first went into hiding. At the beginning of her diary, Anne
would likely never have had the self-insight to make such a sweep-
ing statement. After two years of growth while living in extremely
difficult circumstances, however, she is able to find within herself a
core of hope and optimism. This passage is an example of Anne's
occasional and brilliant glimpses of lucidity and insight into her
horrific situation.

5.   I get cross, then sad, and finally end up turning my
heart inside out, the bad part on the outside and the
good part on the inside, and keep trying to find a way
to become what I'd like to be and what I could be if . . .
if only there were no other people in the world.

This statement ends Anne Frank's last diary entry, written on
August 1, 1944. Anne does not intend to end her diary at this point:
to her, it is just the end of a regular day of hiding in the annex. However, this turns out to be her last entry because the Nazis arrest her
and her family just three days later. It serves as a fitting conclusion
to Anne's development and personal growth during her time in the
annex. Since her time in hiding coincides with puberty, Anne constantly struggles with her identity and her evolving sense of self. She
tries to figure out her role within the annex and how she fits into the
war and suffering in the outside world. Anne believes that she is a
good person, but she also realizes that because of her confinement,
she is unable to reach her true potential until she is released back to
her normal life after the war. Anne's words resonate even more pro-
foundly because we know that within months these "other people"
kill her in the concentration camp. Anne is never allowed to reach
her full potential and never gets the chance to become the good person she has in mind.

KEY FACTS

FULL TITLE
Anne Frank: The Diary of a Young Girl

AUTHOR
Anne Frank

TYPE OF WORK
Diary

GENRE
Diary; historical nonfiction

LANGUAGE
Dutch

TIME AND PLACE WRITTEN
Amsterdam, 1942–1945

DATE OF FIRST PUBLICATION
1947

PUBLISHER
Doubleday

NARRATOR
Anne Frank, a teenage Jewish girl

POINT OF VIEW
Anne speaks in the first person and addresses her diary as a friend. Although she begins writing the diary without any intention of it being read or published, she later writes with the idea that the record of her experiences might be read by others to learn more about the war.

TONE
Anne writes from the perspective of a young girl, so her tone is often emotional and insecure, and she is both critical of herself and others. Her accounts are highly personal and philosophical. She expresses her deep struggle to understand her evolving self, both in relation to her family and to the tumultuous world outside the annex.

TENSE
> Present

SETTING (TIME)
> June 12, 1942–August 1, 1944

SETTING (PLACE)
> Amsterdam, the Netherlands

PROTAGONIST
> Anne Frank

MAJOR CONFLICT
> The perils of living in hiding to escape Nazi persecution of Jewish people; this immediate struggle in Anne's life occurs within the context of the sweeping conflict of World War II

THEMES
> The loneliness of adolescence; the inward versus the outward self; generosity and greed in wartime

MOTIFS
> Becoming a woman; fear

SYMBOLS
> Hanneli; Anne's grandmother

FORESHADOWING
> There is no foreshadowing, since the diary is written in the present tense and Anne had no ability to discern the future. However, constant break-ins, the imprisonment of people who have been providing rations, growing Dutch anti-Semitism, and the probable capture of Anne's friends, including Hanneli, all demonstrate the impending danger that threatens the inhabitants of the annex.

Study Questions & Essay Topics

Study Questions

1. *What role does the diary play in Anne's life?*

When Anne first begins writing in her diary as a thirteen-year-old girl, she feels that her friends and family all misunderstand her. Thus, she first turns to the diary as a new friend and confidant, counting on the diary to be the sympathetic, nonjudgmental ear she has been unable to find elsewhere. Once she goes into hiding in the annex, Anne feels even more misunderstood. She thinks her mother is cold and callous, and feels that the other adults consider her a nuisance. The diary offers Anne much solace in the annex because she is in need of companionship. Until she befriends Peter, Anne has no one other than her diary with whom she can openly share her fear, anger, sadness, and hope. Anne calls the diary "Kitty," indicating that she considers it a close friend. She occasionally even writes to Kitty as if the diary were a person who had asked her questions.

Writing diligently in the diary also helps Anne redirect her strong feelings instead of expressing them outright and causing damage to the fragile relationships within the annex. When everyone around her is feeling anxious and tense, Anne turns to her diary for comfort because she does not want to burden the already overtaxed adults with her own concerns. In this way, Anne becomes very independent at a young age.

Moreover, Anne's constant diary-writing enables her to discover her inner voice and her voice as a writer. The diary gives her a private place to explore and develop her increasingly profound thoughts and ideas. After two years, Anne is able to look back at the invaluable record of her experiences and analyze how she has grown and changed. In this sense, the diary becomes a significant tool for Anne's maturity.

2.   *How does Anne feel about the laws that restrict the
      Jews' freedom?*

The Franks left Germany to live in Holland because they felt they
could escape persecution. After the Germans invaded Holland in
1940, however, the same laws imposed in Germany were extended
to the Netherlands. Anne thinks the laws are unjust, but she does
not completely understand why the Jewish people have been singled
out for this discrimination. She wishes that next time the Jews will
be chosen for something good rather than something bad. Anne
feels it is unfair that Jews cannot use streetcars, that they must wear
yellow stars, and that she must attend a particular school. Nonetheless, she is still optimistic about her family's safety and feels relatively secure about her future. Anne accepts the restrictions as a fact
of life in Amsterdam, and she is thankful to the Dutch people for
their sympathy, especially the ferryman, who lets Jews ride the ferry
because they are not allowed to ride streetcars.

Once the SS call up for Margot, Anne realizes that she is not safe
from the Nazis. Her entire life and worldview is quickly trans-
formed as she is forced into hiding. As Anne hears about more of her
friends being taken to concentration camps, her fears grow and she
questions why the Jews are being restricted. She also questions why
she remains relatively safe while her friends outside have to suffer so
much. Anne says that she does not blame the Dutch people for her
family's misfortune, and her sense of perspective allows her to realize that the non-Jewish Dutch also suffer greatly during the war.
When she hears that the Dutch are becoming more anti-Semitic, she
is disheartened but remains optimistic about humanity.

3.   *Does Anne consider her family lucky or unfortunate to be living in the annex?*

Anne's feelings about the annex constantly change. Most of the time, Anne realizes that she and her family are very fortunate to have the annex as a place to hide. She values the kindness and generosity of her father's non-Jewish colleagues who are risking their lives to provide them with food and supplies. However, Anne often complains about the miserable physical and emotional conditions of the annex, and the confinement bothers her. She misses being able to see nature and the sky and laments that she cannot explore the world. Compared to her formerly comfortable, middle-class life, Anne must live with eight people under severe conditions—she eats rotten potatoes day after day, has no privacy, deals with clashing personalities, and lives in constant fear that the family will be discovered. Most of all, she feels lonely since she has no companions besides Peter in the annex in whom she can confide.

When Anne compares her deprived life to the freedom of non-Jewish Dutch children—a freedom she experienced so recently and took for granted—she feels indignant. However, when she thinks about her Jewish friends and family members who have probably been arrested and sent to concentration camps, such as her friend Hanneli, she feels extremely thankful to still be alive. Anne feels that the Jews as a group are not fortunate and have not been chosen for good things, only bad ones. However, she expresses her conflict over whether she feels fortunate or unlucky about her personal situation. She wonders whether it would have been better to die a quick death than live a confined, tedious, and fearful existence. Anne quickly realizes, however, that she loves life too much and decides she is fortunate that she had the opportunity to evade the Germans.

SUGGESTED ESSAY TOPICS

1.   Why do you think Hanneli appears in Anne's dreams?

2.   Is Anne in love with Peter? Why does she feel she can confide in him?

3.   How is Anne affected by the various break-ins? How is her response connected to her general mood while in hiding?

4.   Do you feel that Anne believes she is going to survive the war? Why or why not?

5.   How does Anne mature and develop through the course of her diary?

REVIEW & RESOURCES

QUIZ

1. Who is Pim?

    A. Anne's father
    B. The cat
    C. Peter
    D. Mr. van Daan

2. What does Albert Dussel do for a living before he goes into hiding?

    A. He is a doctor
    B. He is a dentist
    C. He writes books
    D. He sells pharmaceuticals

3. What does Anne receive for her thirteenth birthday?

    A. A pony
    B. A fountain pen
    C. A bicycle
    D. A diary

4. What group are the Franks hiding from?

    A. The Nazis
    B. The Belgian Army
    C. The Allies
    D. The French

5. What is the Gestapo?

    A. The German secret police
    B. The Dutch Army
    C. A concentration camp
    D. A law preventing the Jews from holding jobs

6.   Why doesn't Mr. Dussel's wife join them in hiding?

    A.   She is not Jewish
    B.   They were recently divorced
    C.   The Gestapo have already captured her
    D.   She wants to emigrate to France

7.   Who is Peter's mother?

    A.   Bep
    B.   Mrs. Dussel
    C.   Mrs. van Daan
    D.   Miep Gies

8.   What is D-Day?

    A.   The day the Allied troops land in France
    B.   The first day of the war
    C.   The last day of the war
    D.   The day Auschwitz opens

9.   Who eventually publishes Anne's diary?

    A.   Bep
    B.   Her father
    C.   Miep
    D.   Peter

10.   What friend of Anne's shows up in one of her dreams?

    A.   Peter
    B.   Hanneli
    C.   Margot
    D.   Bep

11.   What does Anne call her diary?

    A.   Margot
    B.   Ms.
    C.   Beatrice
    D.   Kitty

12. What does Anne want to be when she grows up?

    A. A dentist
    B. President
    C. A doctor
    D. A writer

13. Who gives Anne her first kiss?

    A. Jan
    B. Peter van Daan
    C. Albert
    D. Peter Schiff

14. Who is Margot?

    A. Anne's sister
    B. Anne's mother
    C. Anne's cat
    D. Anne's best friend

15. What are ration coupons used for?

    A. Buying food
    B. Distributing weapons
    C. Receiving messages about the war
    D. Identifying Jews

16. What symbol are Jews required to wear during the Nazi occupation?

    A. The Star of David
    B. The letter J
    C. A red cross
    D. The German flag

17. Why does Anne not ride any streetcars?

    A. They are too hot
    B. They are too crowded
    C. Jews are forbidden on streetcars
    D. She dislikes them

REVIEW & RESOURCES

18. Who is Bep?

    A.   A secretary who helped to hide the Franks
    B.   Anne's sister
    C.   Anne's cat
    D.   A teacher who gave Anne the diary

19. Where was Anne born?

    A.   London, England
    B.   Frankfurt, Germany
    C.   Amsterdam, the Netherlands
    D.   Paris, France

20. How many people ultimately live in the annex?

    A.   Four
    B.   Five
    C.   Eight
    D.   Ten

21. Why did the Franks tell people they were going to Switzerland?

    A.   To confuse Mr. Frank's creditors
    B.   To make the Nazis think they were in Switzerland
    C.   They planned on going to Switzerland but had to stay in the annex instead
    D.   They wanted Mr. Frank's sister to think they were in Switzerland

22. To which concentration camp was Anne sent?

    A.   Auschwitz
    B.   Dachau
    C.   Bergen-Belsen
    D.   Goebbels

23. By the conclusion of the diary, Anne believes that people are fundamentally

    A. Good
    B. Evil
    C. Greedy
    D. Jealous

24. Which of Anne's relatives survived the Holocaust?

    A. Her mother
    B. Her grandmother
    C. Her father
    D. Her sister

25. What does Anne hope to ask Peter about?

    A. The meaning of life
    B. The songs on the radio
    C. The fate of the Jews
    D. The female genitalia

ANSWER KEY:
1: A; 2: B; 3: D; 4: A; 5: A; 6: A; 7: C; 8: A; 9: B; 10: B;
11: D; 12: D; 13: B; 14: A; 15: A; 16: A; 17: C; 18: A; 19: B;
20: C; 21: B; 22: C; 23: A; 24: C; 25: D

SUGGESTIONS FOR FURTHER READING

BARNOUW, DAVID AND GERALD VAN DER STROOM, eds. *The Diary of Anne Frank: The Critical Edition*. New York: Doubleday, 1989.

GIES, MIEP AND ALISON LESLIE GOLD. *Anne Frank Remembered: The Story of the Woman Who Helped to Hide the Frank Family*. New York: Simon and Schuster Trade Paperbacks, 1987.

LEVIN, MEYER. *Anne Frank: A Play*. M. Levin, 1967.

RITTNER, CAROL, ED. *Anne Frank in the World, 1929–1945*. New York: M.E. Sharpe, 1998.

SCHNABEL, ERNST. *Anne Frank: A Portrait in Courage*. New York: Harcourt Brace, 1958.

VAN GALEN LAST, D. *Anne Frank and After*. Amsterdam: Amsterdam University Press, 1996.

VAN DER ROL, RUUD. *Anne Frank: Beyond the Diary*. New York: Viking, 1993.

REVIEW & RESOURCES

A Note on the Type

The typeface used in SparkNotes study guides is Sabon, created by master typographer Jan Tschichold in 1964. Tschichold revolutionized the field of graphic design twice: first with his use of asymmetrical layouts and sanserif type in the 1930s when he was affiliated with the Bauhaus, then by abandoning assymetry and calling for a return to the classic ideals of design. Sabon, his only extant typeface, is emblematic of his latter program: Tschichold's design is a recreation of the types made by Claude Garamond, the great French typographer of the Renaissance, and his contemporary Robert Granjon. Fittingly, it is named for Garamond's apprentice, Jacques Sabon.

SparkNotes
Test Preparation
Guides

The SparkNotes team figured it was time to cut standardized tests down to size. We've studied the tests for you, so that SparkNotes test prep guides are:

Smarter
Packed with critical-thinking skills and test-
taking strategies that will improve your score.

Better
Fully up to date, covering all new features of the tests,
with study tips on every type of question.

Faster
Our books cover exactly what you need to
know for the test. No more, no less.

SparkNotes Guide to the SAT & PSAT
SparkNotes Guide to the SAT & PSAT — Deluxe Internet Edition
SparkNotes Guide to the ACT
SparkNotes Guide to the ACT — Deluxe Internet Edition
SparkNotes SAT Verbal Workbook
SparkNotes SAT Math Workbook
SparkNotes Guide to the SAT II Writing
5 More Practice Tests for the SAT II Writing
SparkNotes Guide to the SAT II U.S. History
5 More Practice Tests for the SAT II History
SparkNotes Guide to the SAT II Math Ic
5 More Practice Tests for the SAT II Math Ic
SparkNotes Guide to the SAT II Math IIc
5 More Practice Tests for the SAT II Math IIc
SparkNotes Guide to the SAT II Biology
5 More Practice Tests for the SAT II Biology
SparkNotes Guide to the SAT II Physics

SPARKNOTES™ LITERATURE GUIDES